FUNNY TRICKS AND PRACTICAL JOKES

TO PLAY ON YOUR FRIENDS

BY ALESHA SULLIVAN

CAPSTONE PRESS
a capstone imprint

Blazers Books are published by Capstone Press,
1710 Roe Crest Drive, North Mankato, Minnesota 56003
www.mycapstone.com

Library of Congress Cataloging-in-Publication Data
Library of Congress Cataloging-in-Publication data is available on the Library of
Congress website.
ISBN 978-1-5435-0340-1 (library binding)
ISBN 978-1-5435-0349-4 (eBook PDF)

Editorial Credits:
Mandy Robbins, editor; Eric Gohl, media researcher; Sarah Schuette, photo stylist;
Marcy Morin, scheduler; Tori Abraham, production specialist

Photo Credits:
All photographs by Capstone Studio/Karon Dubke

Printed and bound in the United States of America.
010877S18

TABLE OF CONTENTS

HOW TO PULL THE PERFECT PRANK

Do you get a good laugh from playing tricks on your friends? Who doesn't? If you're a prankster, these easy and funny gags are sure to keep your friends off balance.

HOW TO BE A PERFECT PRANKSTER

- Choose the right target or audience. Pick people with a sense of humor.

- Choose the right time and place. For example, don't do pranks at school.

- Be responsible. Don't pull pranks that are dangerous, hurtful, or destructive.

- After playing a prank, admit to being the prankster. Then be sure to clean up any messes made.

COOKIE SURPRISE!

Serve up an unexpected sandwich cookie! Play a savory trick on your friends with some crème-filled cookies and hummus. Your friends will be in for a surprising dose of protein.

What You Need:

- 1 package of sandwich-crème cookies
- butter knife
- white bean hummus

6

What You Do:

1. Carefully pull apart the crème cookies.

2. Use the butter knife to gently scrape off the crème filling.

3. Replace the crème filling with a layer of white bean hummus.

4. Put the cookies back together.

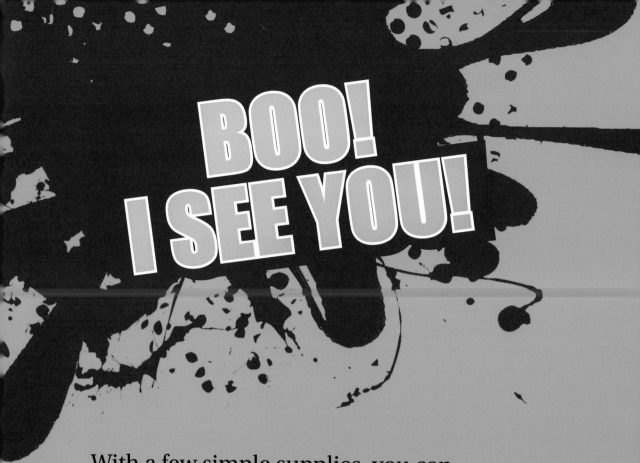

BOO! I SEE YOU!

With a few simple supplies, you can play a trick on your entire family. Boo! The food in the fridge is staring back at you!

What You Need:

- googly eyes of different sizes
- scissors
- double-sided tape

What You Do:

1. Cut small circles of tape and attach to the backsides of the googly eyes.

2. Place the googly eyes on various items in the refrigerator when no one is looking.

TIP! Get creative! Use some felt to add tongues, eyebrows, or ears to your refrigerator friends.

UNDRINKABLE DRINKS

Your friends will be excited to gulp down this delicious juice. Until they realize it's undrinkable, that is! This juice is actually gelatin, making it impossible to chug.

What You Need:

- 1 package of red gelatin
- a measuring cup
- 3 cups distilled water
- whisk
- clear cups or glasses
- drinking straws

What You Do:

1. Prepare the gelatin according to package instructions.

2. Carefully pour the liquid gelatin into clear cups.

3. Place a drinking straw into each cup.

4. Place the cups in the refrigerator to allow the gelatin to set.

5. Surprise your friends with their undrinkable drinks!

CAUTION!

Have an adult help when preparing the gelatin and using boiling water.

RAT PROBLEM

Rats — we have a rodent problem! Freak out your friends with a beetroot that looks like a huge, gross rat. Be prepared to cover your ears for all the screams!

What You Need:

- beetroot with a long root still attached
- sharp knife
- cereal or snack box

What You Do:

1. Cut the bottom of the beetroot with the knife so it lays flat.

2. Place a cereal or snack box on its side. Then place the beetroot inside so the long root faces outward.

TIP! Ask an adult to help when using the sharp knife.

EGGS-SCUSE ME!

Do you want to give someone a chuckle with breakfast? Give the eggs in your refrigerator a little personality.

What You Need:

- permanent markers
- a carton of eggs

What You Do:

1. Use the markers to draw terrified faces on the eggs. You could include fake "cracks" in their heads.

2. Ask your parent or caregiver to make eggs for breakfast. Watch them gasp and giggle when they open the carton.

TIP! You could add a word bubble that reads, "Don't eat me!"

SPONGE BROWNIES

Imagine seeing a really tasty
chocolate-frosted brownie. You take a
big bite and . . . yuck! The brownie looks
real, but it sure doesn't taste like it!

What You Need:

- scissors
- 1 dry kitchen sponge
- butter knife
- chocolate frosting
- sprinkles (optional)

What You Do:

1. Cut the sponge in half using the scissors.

2. Use the butter knife to spread chocolate frosting all over the sponge squares. Make sure all sides are well-covered, except the bottoms.

3. Add some sprinkles, and wait for someone to take a bite!

TIP!

Be extra sneaky by including one or two "sponge brownies" on a plate of real brownies. Bad luck can decide who gets the spongy treats!

BUGS EVERYWHERE!

Give your friends a creepy surprise.
First get creative with creepy crawlies.
Then watch your friends jump in fear
when they turn on the lights!

What You Need:

- pencil
- bug or insect stencils
- black construction paper
- scissors
- tape

What You Do:

1. Trace the shapes of big bugs onto the black construction paper.

2. Cut out the bugs with the scissors.

3. Tape the fake bugs inside a lamp shade or ceiling light.

T. P. IN THE SHOE

Are your friends' feet growing? Or are their shoes shrinking? Pull this trick on all your friends and they'll think their feet grew overnight!

What You Need:

- toilet paper or tissues
- several of your friends' shoes

What You Do:

1. Make sure your friends aren't nearby.

2. Place balled up toilet paper or tissues inside the toes of their shoes. Be sure the tissue isn't visible.

3. Laugh and watch while they try to put their shoes on!

ICE CUBE CRITTERS

Want to freak out your family at dinner time? This oldie but goodie is easy to do. And it's sure to scare the appetite out of your victims.

What You Need:

- ice cube tray
- water
- small fake bugs or insects
- clear cups or glasses
- water or juice

What You Do:

1. Fill an ice cube tray with water.

2. Slide the fake bugs into each cube slot in the tray.

3. Place the tray in the freezer.

4. At mealtime offer to pour the drinks. Place several ice cubes into each cup. Then add water or juice.

5. Get ready to watch your family and friends squirm!

SOMETHING'S WRONG WITH THE SINK

"What's wrong with the water?" Your friends will get a shock when crazy colored water pours from the faucet. The color lasts only a few seconds, but this trick will leave everyone laughing!

What You Need:

- cotton swab
- nontoxic, gel food coloring

What You Do:

1. Use the cotton swab to smear gel food coloring inside the faucet of the sink.

2. Ask your friend to turn the water on to get you a glass of water.

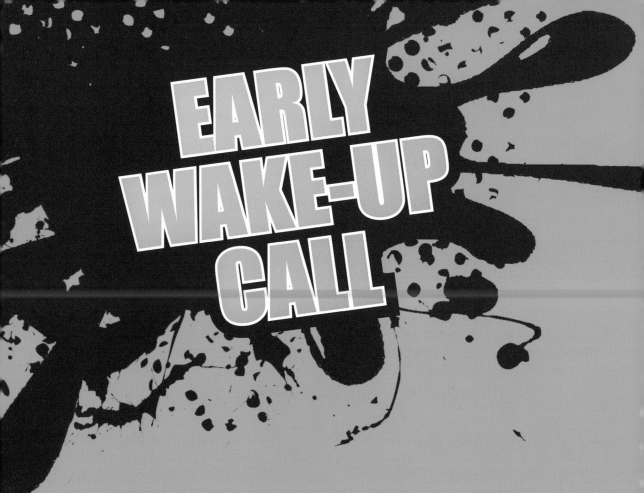

EARLY WAKE-UP CALL

Looking for a simple trick to play on someone? Use this one to give your friend an extra-early wake-up call! However — you may want to sleep on the opposite side of the house!

What You Need:

- radio alarm clock

What You Do:

1. Make sure your victim has an alarm clock. When he or she isn't in the room, figure out how to set the alarm.

2. Set the alarm for early in the morning, such as 4:00 a.m. Turn the volume up extra loud.

3. Sit back and relax while he or she wakes up too early. Warning: your friend might be really cranky that day!

READ MORE

Elliot, Rob. *Laugh-Out-Loud Road Trip Jokes for Kids.* Laugh-Out-Loud Jokes For Kids. New York: HarperCollins, 2017.

Lewis, J. Patrick. *Just Joking: Animal Riddles.* National Geographic Kids. Washington, D.C.: National Geographic, 2015.

Yoe, Craig. *LOL: A Load of Laughs for Kids.* New York: Little Simon, 2017.

INTERNET SITES

Use FactHound to find Internet sites related to this book.

Visit *www.facthound.com*

Just type in 9781543503401 and go.

 Check out projects, games and lots more at
www.capstonekids.com